Bandit

Carliss Cline

To order additional copies of this book, contact:
Xlibris Corporation
1-888-795-4274
www.Xlibris.com
Orders@Xlibris.com

This is a true story about a raccoon named Bandit. He was abandoned from his family at early age and needed a loving home. Someone to care for him and protect him.

This is how I became Bandits mother. As you read this short story, you will learn about Bandits everyday life as he grows up. I think you will enjoy these experiences we share as much as I have.

This is Bandit when he first arrived at his new home. At this age he likes to eat and sleep.

Bandit is playing with his toys but he will be hungry soon.

Bandit loves feeding time. He is ready for his bottle of milk and apple sauce. At this time Bandit eats every two or three hours.

Bandit has gotten older so he sleeps outside. He may sleep in a box with towels, a pile of wood or most anywhere its dark and quiet. He may even try to climb a tree

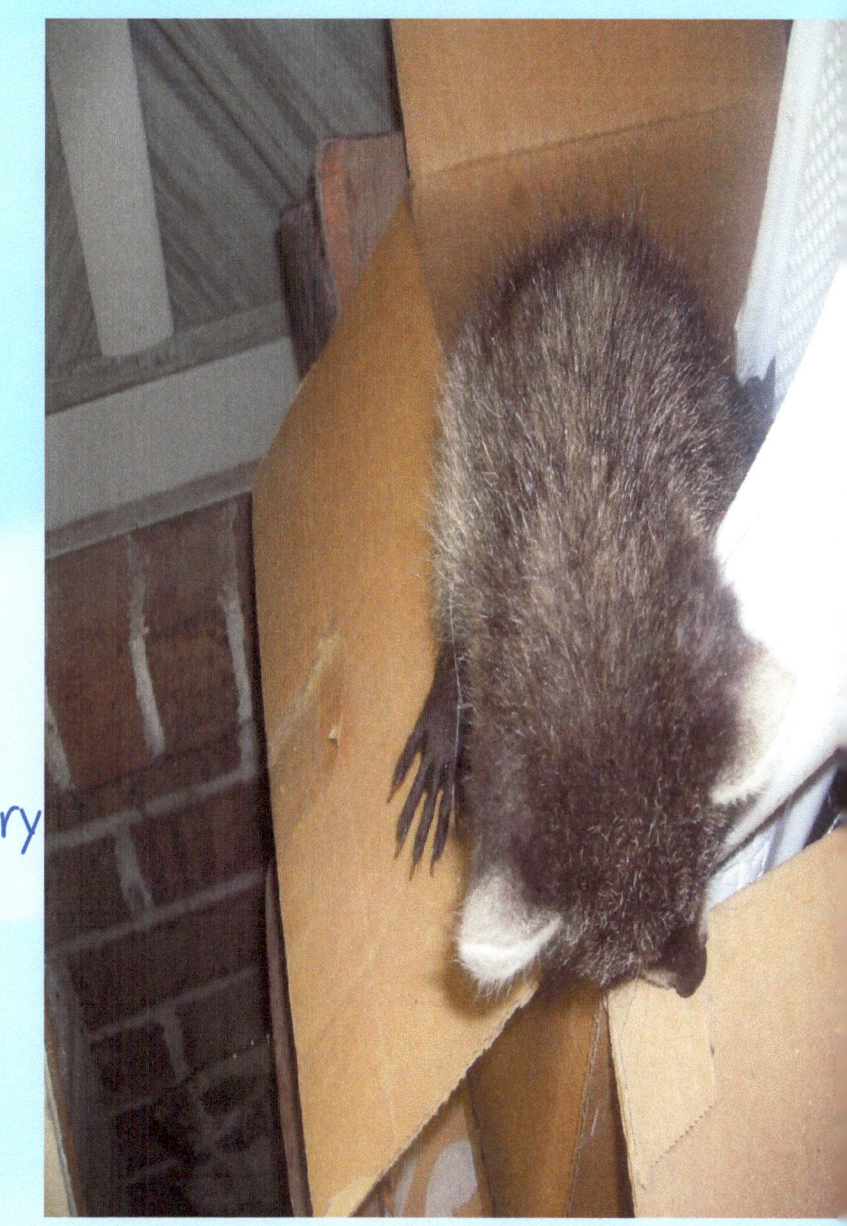

Bandit likes playing with ice cubes. He will take them out of his bowl one at a time until his bowl is empty.

By the way in case you don't know raccoons are grayish brown American mammal that has a fox like face with a black mask, and a ring tail.

Bandit likes taking walks around the yard while I water the bushes. He plays in the water and digs in the dirt. It is cooling off time.

This is Bandit cooling off

Bandit is trying to climb a tree. He is still a little afraid and clumsy. He is not to sure of himself yet.

As Bandit gets older, he likes to suck on your arms, hands, feet or even your legs. He is not trying to bite. He is merely using you as a pacifier. It does not hurt, but feels a bit funny to your skin. This sucking is soothing and they will usually do this to the main person feeding them.

Bandit likes attention and not always does he like being held. Sometimes he likes to be the aggressive one. Bandit will crawl up the door when he wants in the house. Let me in! Ready or not.

Bandits way of saying, I'm coming in!

Bandit is persistent, very curious and likes to keep busy. He needs objects to occupy his time. Today he is going horse back riding.

Again Bandit is playing around the bushes. This is his everyday event. I believe this is his favorite routine of the day following me from one bush to another.

Bandit likes digging.

Bandit likes to play with his best friend Marlee. She is a Chihuahua and full of fun. Bandit also has a few other friends he enjoys playing with. Mollyanna a little Yorkie and Zeus another Chihuahua.

Who is going to make the first move?

Bandit and his friend I'lene

I know one day when Bandit gets older he will wander off with other raccoons. I will miss him and all the good times we shared. I have to remember he belongs in the wild and one day he will return to his own habitat. I will always be looking and hoping for a visit from him.

Bandit running from me

Bandit playing with

the running water

Bandit riding his horse.

To sum it up Bandit is much like a two year old. He gets into everything. We still play every night on the front porch while everyone else is sleeping. Bandit did learn to climb and he is very independent, but still likes his

"MOMMY".

The End

www.ingramcontent.com/pod-product-compliance
Lightning Source LLC
Chambersburg PA
CBHW060817290526
45792CB00005BB/1689